D1083733

JAN   2011

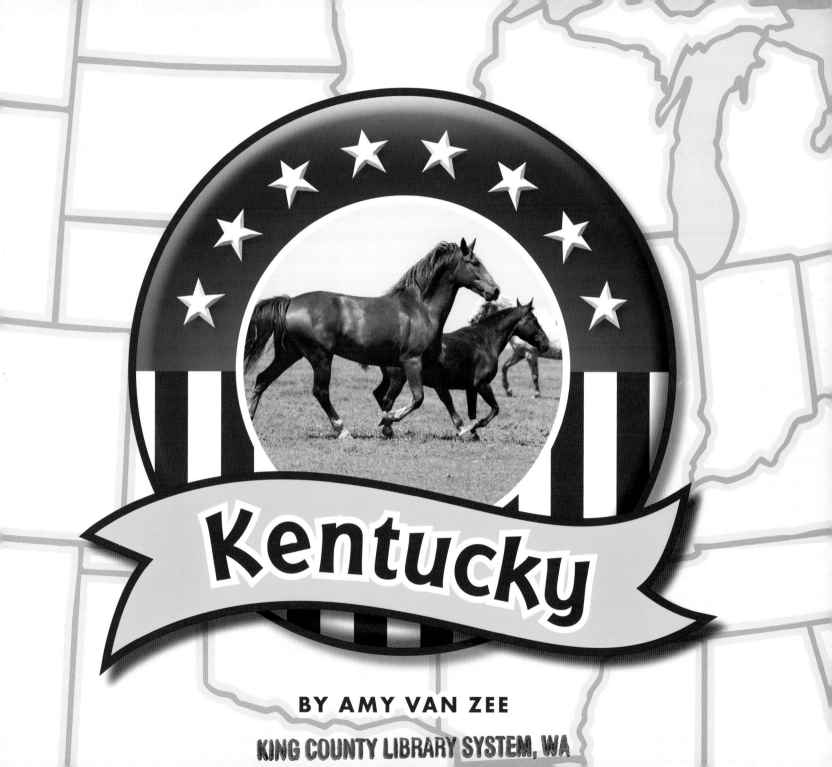

Kentucky

BY AMY VAN ZEE

Published by The Child's World®
1980 Lookout Drive • Mankato, MN 56003-1705
800-599-READ • www.childsworld.com

ACKNOWLEDGMENTS
The Child's World®: Mary Berendes, Publishing Director
The Design Lab: Design and production
Red Line Editorial: Editorial direction

PHOTO CREDITS: iStockphoto, cover, 1, 3, 9, 10, 11, 13; Matt Kania/Map
Hero, Inc., 4, 5; Todd Taulman/iStockphoto, 7; North Wind Picture Archives/
Photolibrary, 15; Anne Kitzman/Shutterstock Images, 17; AP Images, 19; Al
Behrman/AP Images, 21; One Mile Up, 22; Quarter-dollar coin image from
the United States Mint, 22

LIBRARY OF CONGRESS CATALOGING-IN-PUBLICATION DATA
Van Zee, Amy.
  Kentucky / by Amy Van Zee.
      p. cm.
  Includes bibliographical references and index.
  ISBN 978-1-60253-461-2 (library bound : alk. paper)
  1. Kentucky—Juvenile literature. I. Title.

F451.3.V37 2010
976.9—dc22

                              2010017713

Printed in the United States of America in Mankato, Minnesota.
July 2010
F11538

On the cover:
Some people
in Kentucky
breed horses.

CONTENTS

Geography

Let's explore Kentucky! Kentucky is in the east-central United States.

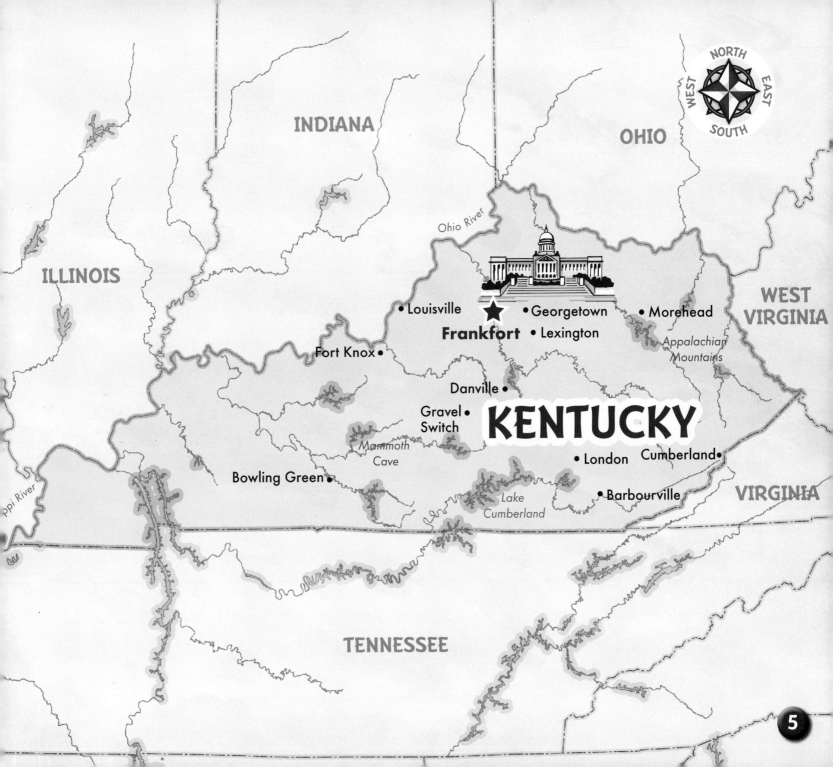

NORTH
WEST EAST
SOUTH

INDIANA

OHIO

ILLINOIS

Ohio River

WEST
VIRGINIA

• Louisville

• Georgetown

• Morehead

Frankfort

• Lexington

Appalachian
Mountains

Fort Knox •

Danville •

Gravel
Switch •

KENTUCKY

Mammoth
Cave

• London

Cumberland •

Bowling Green •

Lake
Cumberland

• Barbourville

VIRGINIA

ppi River

TENNESSEE

Cities

Frankfort is the capital of Kentucky.
Louisville is the largest city in the state.
Lexington is another large city.

Louisville sits along the Ohio River. ▶

Land

Kentucky has mountains, valleys, rivers, lakes, and streams. The Ohio River makes up the northern border of the state. The Mississippi River is its western border. Parts of the Appalachian Mountains are in the east.

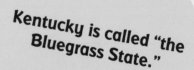

Kentucky is called "the Bluegrass State."

Lake Cumberland is Kent
Many people go

9

Plants and Animals

Almost half of Kentucky is forests. The state tree is the tulip poplar. It is also known as the yellow poplar. Kentucky's state flower is the goldenrod. It grows in the wild in Kentucky. The state bird is the cardinal.

Goldenrods bloom in the summer and fall. ▶

People and Work

More than 4.2 million people live in Kentucky. In Kentucky, many people live in **urban** areas. Farming and coal mining are important jobs in the state.

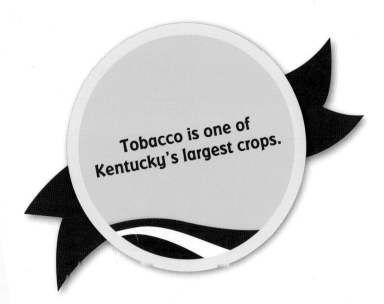

Tobacco is one of Kentucky's largest crops.

A worker in a coal mine prepares to drive a truck full of coal ▶

History

Native Americans have lived in the Kentucky area for thousands of years. Explorers from Europe came to this land in the 1600s and 1700s. Daniel Boone came to the area in 1767. Settlers and Native Americans fought over the land. In 1776, Kentucky became part of Virginia. But Kentucky split and became the fifteenth state on June 1, 1792.

Daniel Boone explored and settled in what is now Kentucky. ▶

Ways of Life

Kentucky has trails for **hiking** and lakes for boating and fishing. Many people like to watch horse races, too. There are many national parks to explore. People in Kentucky can visit **museums** and **theaters**.

Warm summer days in Kentucky are good for boating. ▶

Famous People

Abraham Lincoln was born in Kentucky. He was the sixteenth president of the United States. Jefferson Davis was born here, too. He led the South during the U.S. **Civil War**. Television **journalist** Diane Sawyer and boxer Muhammad Ali were also born in Kentucky.

Some people think Muhammad Ali (standing) was one of the best boxers of all time. ▶

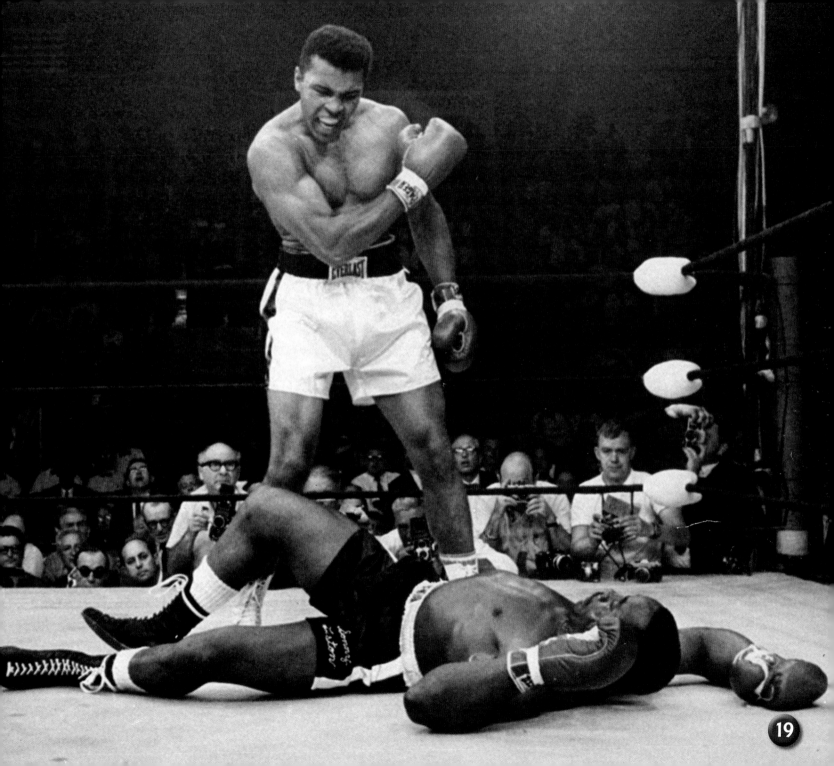

Famous Places

Mammoth Cave is a large national park in south-central Kentucky. It contains more than 360 miles (579 km) of caves. Churchill Downs is in Louisville. This famous racetrack hosts the Kentucky Derby. This horse race is held every year.

Thousands of people come to Churchill Downs ▶ to watch the Kentucky Derby each year.

21

State Symbols

Seal
The Kentucky state seal shows two people shaking hands. It stands for the state **motto**, "United We Stand, Divided We Fall." Go to childsworld.com/links for a link to Kentucky's state Web site, where you can get a firsthand look at the state seal.

Flag
The state flag has the seal on it. Goldenrod flowers surround the seal.

Quarter
A racehorse is on the Kentucky state quarter. The quarter came out in 2001.

Glossary

breed (BREED): To breed is to keep animals together to produce young. Some people in Kentucky breed horses.

Civil War (SIV-il WOR): In the United States, the Civil War was a war fought between the Northern and the Southern states from 1861 to 1865. The leader of the South during the Civil War was born in Kentucky.

hiking (HYK-ing): Hiking is taking a walk in a natural area, such as a hill or a mountain. People enjoy hiking in Kentucky.

journalist (JUR-nul-ist): A journalist is a person who collects and reports news. Journalist Diane Sawyer is from Kentucky.

motto (MOT-oh): A motto is a sentence that states what people stand for or believe. Kentucky's motto is "United We Stand, Divided We Fall."

museums (myoo-ZEE-umz): Museums are places where people go to see art, history, or science displays. People in Kentucky visit museums.

seal (SEEL): A seal is a symbol a state uses for government business. Kentucky's seal shows two friends hugging.

symbols (SIM-bulz): Symbols are pictures or things that stand for something else. The seal and flag are Kentucky's symbols.

theaters (thee-IT-urz): Theaters are buildings where movies and plays are shown. People in Kentucky enjoy going to theaters.

urban (URR-bun): Urban relates to city life. Many people live in Kentucky's urban areas.

Further Information

Books

McCabe Riehle, Mary Ann. *B is for Bluegrass: A Kentucky Alphabet*. Chelsea, MI: Sleeping Bear Press, 2002.

Reynolds, Jeff. *A to Z: United States of America*. New York: Children's Press, 2005.

Valzania, Kimberly. *Kentucky*. New York: Children's Press, 2003.

Web Sites

Visit our Web site for links about Kentucky: *childsworld.com/links*

Note to Parents, Teachers, and Librarians: We routinely verify our Web links to make sure they are safe and active sites. So encourage your readers to check them out!

Index